AUTHENTIC TRANSCRIPTIONS
WITH NOTES AND TABLATURE

**Transcribed by
JESSE GRESS**

eric clapton

from the album
eric clapton unplugged

ISBN 0-7935-2084-3

7777 W. BLUEMOUND RD. P.O. BOX 13819 MILWAUKEE, WI 53213

eric clapton
from the album
eric clapton unplugged
contents

Alberta

Words and Music by Huddie Ledbetter

8

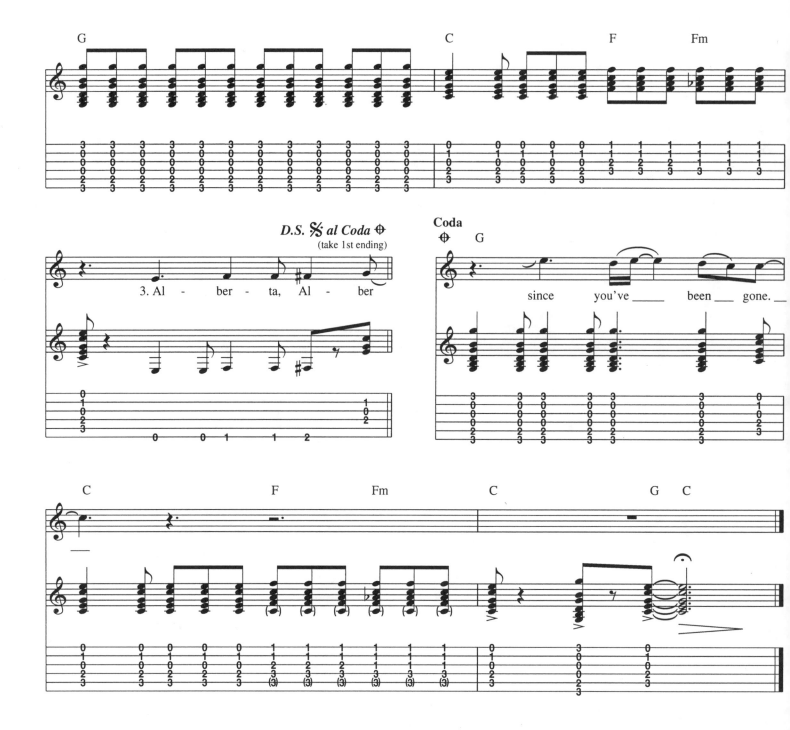

Additional lyrics

2. Alberta, Alberta, where'd you stay last night?
   Alberta, Alberta, where'd you stay last night?
   Come home this mornin', clothes don't fit you right.

3. Alberta, Alberta, girl you're on my mind.
   Alberta, Alberta, girl you're on my mind.
   Ain't had no lovin' in such a great, long time.

4. Alberta, Alberta, where you been so long?
   Alberta, Alberta, where you been so long?
   Ain't had no lovin' since you've been gone.

Before You Accuse Me

Words and Music by Eugene McDaniels

5th Verse

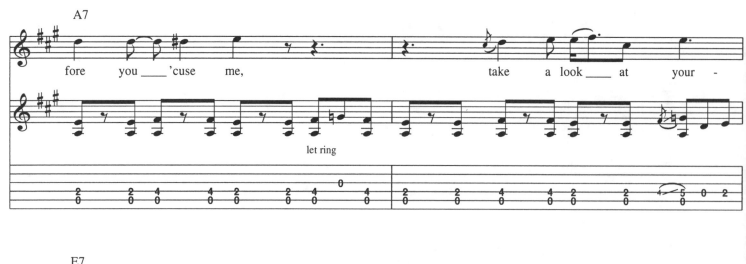

fore you ____ 'cuse me, take a look ____ at your -

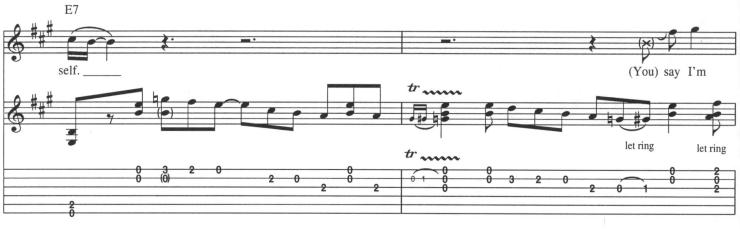

self. _____ (You) say I'm

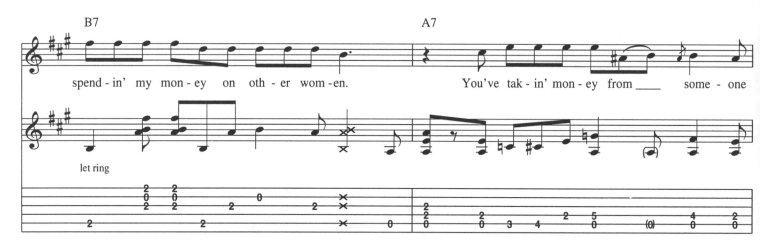

spend - in' my mon - ey on oth - er wom - en. You've tak - in' mon - ey from ____ some - one

else.

18

2nd Guitar Solo

Hey Hey

By William "Big Bill" Broonzy

Intro

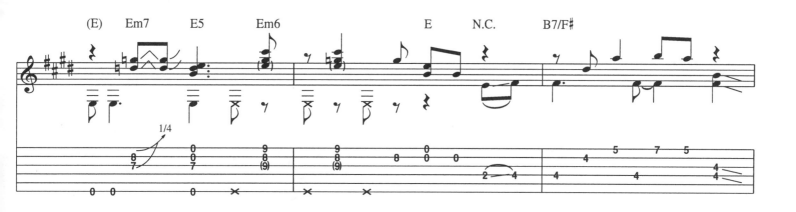

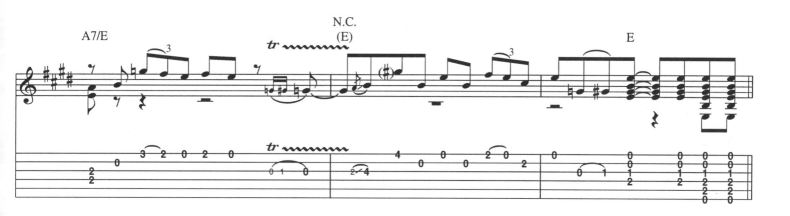

2nd Verse

Hey, hey, ___ hey, hey ___ ba - by, hey. _____

Layla

Words and Music by Eric Clapton and Jim Gordon

2nd and 3rd Verses

2. Tried to give you con-sol-a-tion, __ your old man had let you

3. Make the best of the sit-u-a-tion, __ before I fin-ally go in-

down. __ Like _ a _ fool, I fall in love _ with you.

sane. __ Please _ don't say we'll nev-er find __ a way.

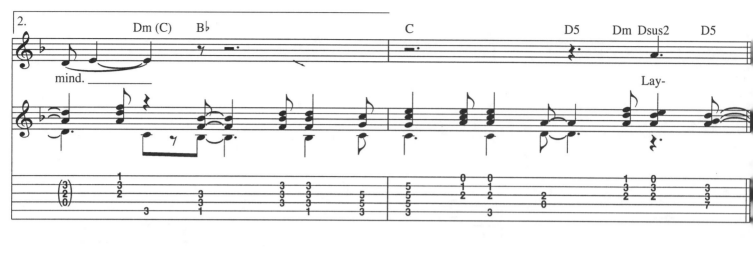

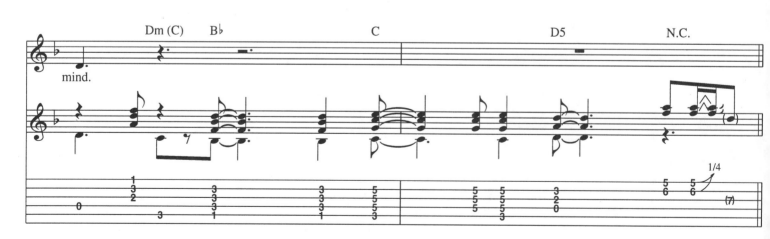

Guitar Solo

Malted Milk
Words and Music by Robert Johnson

Intro

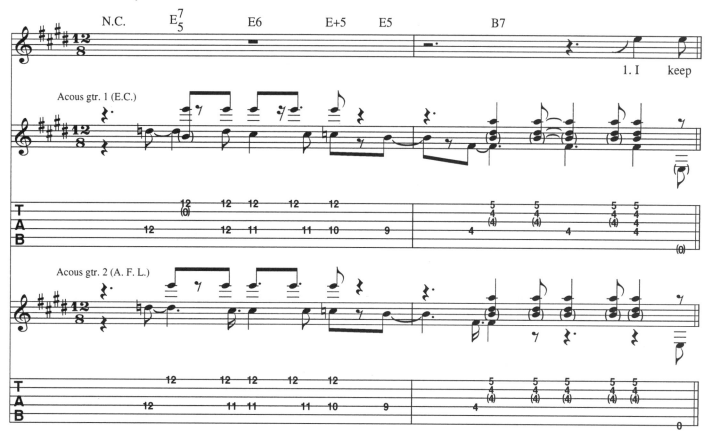

my malt-ed milk, ma-ma, ___ un - til I change my mind. ___

Guitar Solo

even release

snap string   snap string

Lonely Stranger

Words and Music by Eric Clapton

1st, 2nd, 3rd, 4th Verses

1. I must be _____ in - vis - i - ble. _____ No one knows _____ me. _____
(2, 3, 4, *See additional lyrics.*)

I have crawled _____ down dead end streets _____

on my hands _____ and knees. _____

* T on ⑥

* T = thumb

45

Yes, ___ I will.

Yes, ___ I

will. _____

Yes, ___ I ___ will. _____

Yes, I will. _____

snap string

let ring

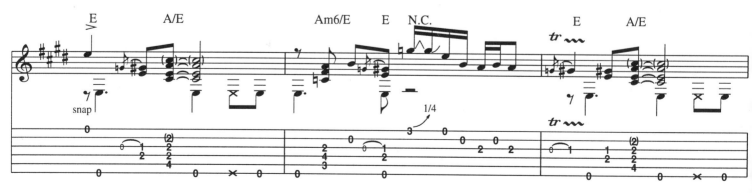

snap

1/4

Additional Lyrics

2. I was born with a raging thirst,
   A hunger to be free.
   But I've learned through the years,
   Don't encourage me.

3. When I walk, stay behind,
   Don't get close to me.
   'Cause it's sure to end in tears,
   So just let me be.

4. Some will say that I'm no good,
   Maybe I agree.
   Take a look, then walk away,
   That's alright with me.

Nobody Knows You When You're Down and Out

Words and Music by Jimmy Cox

I said it straight _ with-out an-y doubt, no-bod-y knows you when you're down _

even ♪'s ----------- **Guitar Solo**

_ and _ out.

w/pick *f*

Piano Solo

finger style
mf

snap string

let ring ---------------

Old Love

Words and Music by Eric Clapton and Robert Cray

* Bass gtr. plays D throughout chords.

62

Rollin' and Tumblin'

Written by Muddy Waters

Moderately fast ♩ = 122

1st Verse

Well, I woke up this morn-

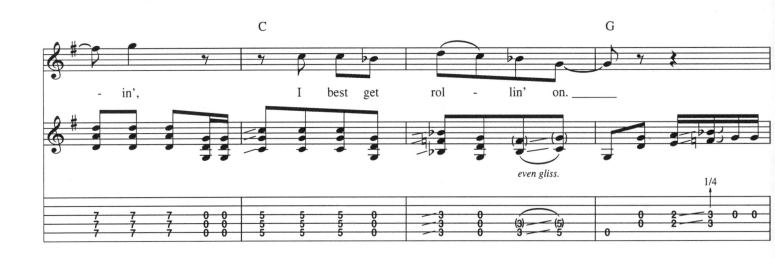

-in', I best get rol - lin' on. _____

even gliss.

2nd Verse

2. Well now, come here ba - by,

sit down on dad - dy's knee. _____

Well now, come here ba-

Guitar solo

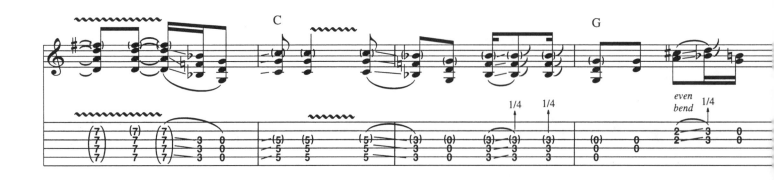

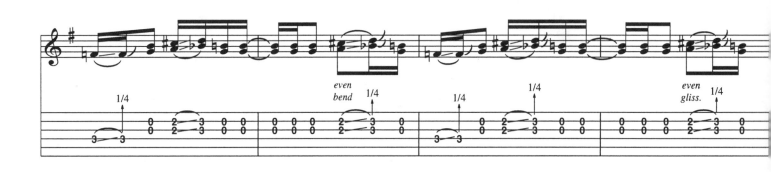

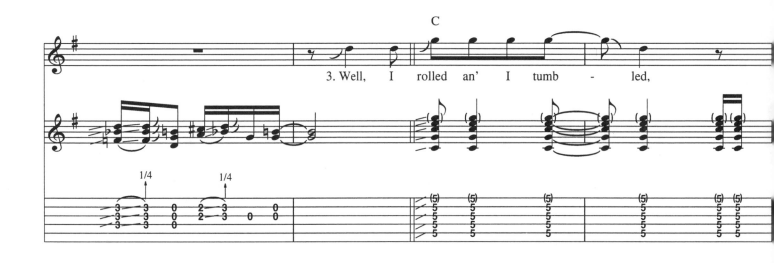

3. Well, I rolled an' I tumb - led,

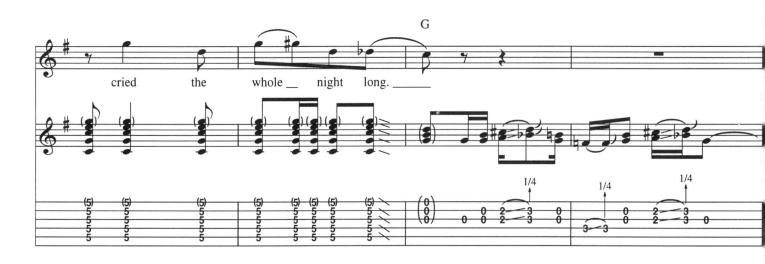

cried the whole __ night long. _____

4th Verse

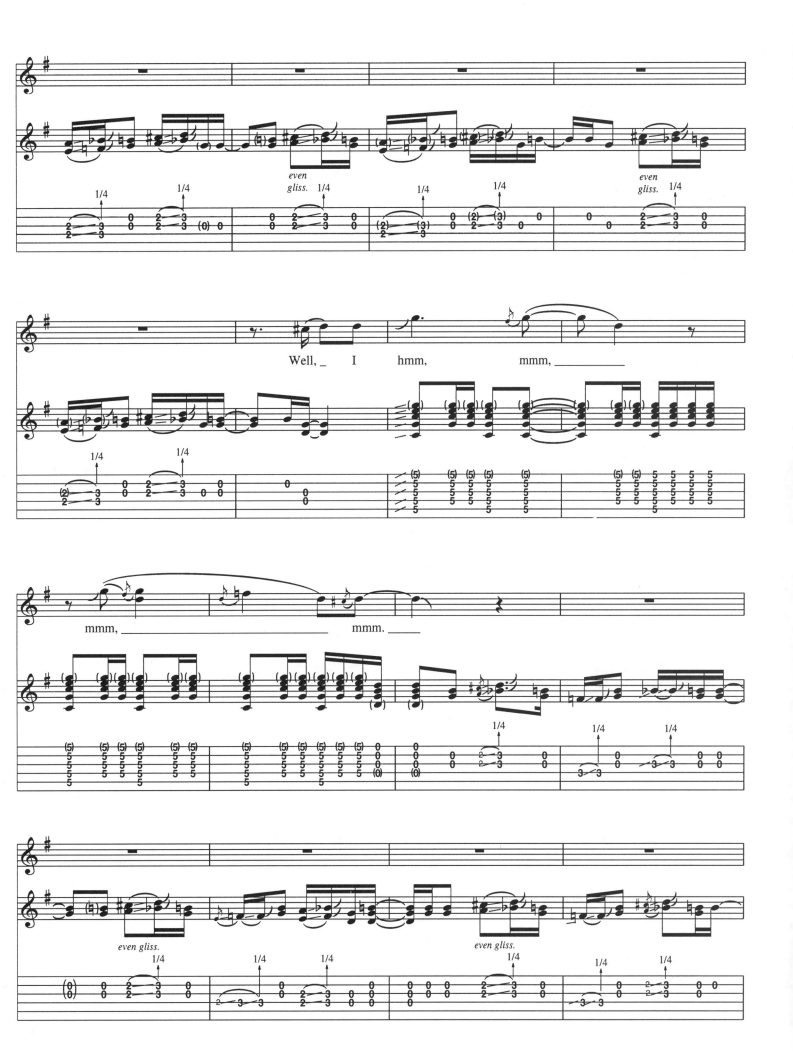

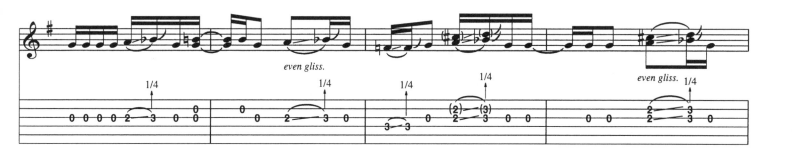

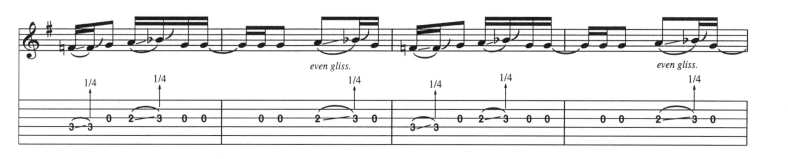

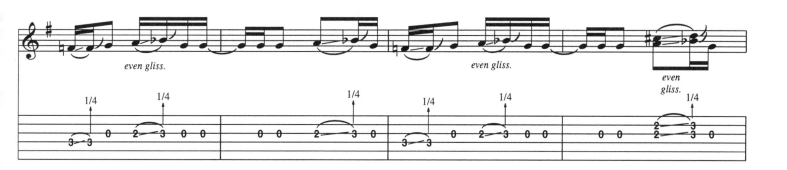

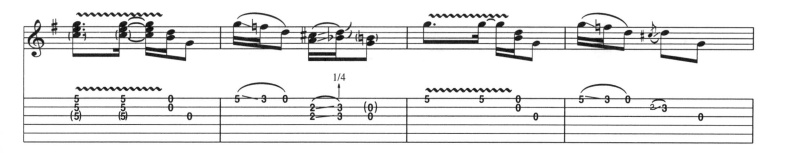

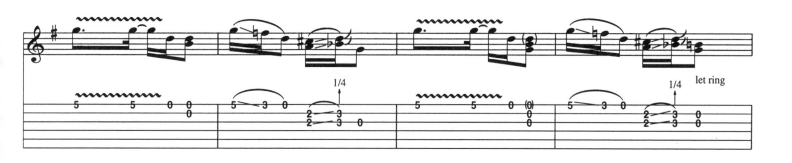

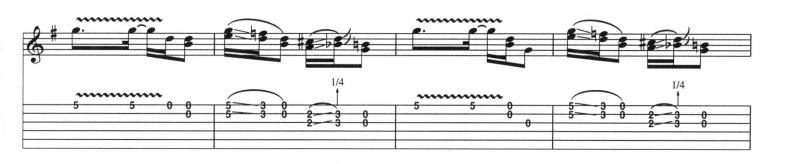

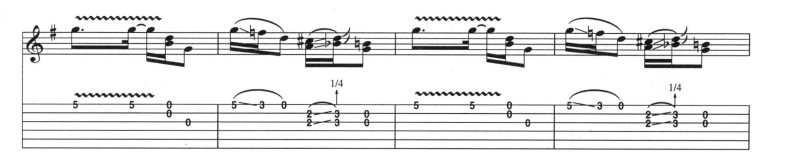

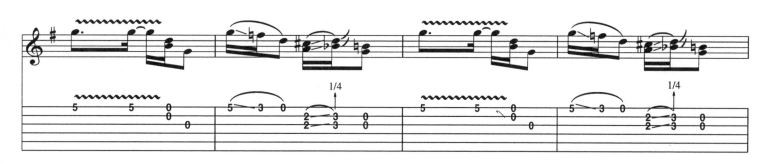

Running On Faith

Words and Music by Jerry Lynn Williams

Signe

Words and Music by Eric Clapton

Intro

Moderately fast bossa nova feel ♩ = 176

Tears In Heaven

Words and Music by Eric Clapton and Will Jennings

Walkin' Blues

Words and Music by Robert Johnson

1st Verse

Guitar Solo

3rd Verse

3. Peo - ple tell me ___ the walk-in' blues ain't bad. ___ The worse old feel - in'

I most ___ ev - er had. _____ Peo - ple tell me the old walk-in' blues ain't bad.

Well, it's the worse old feel - in',

woo _ Lord, the most _ I ev- er had. ___

102

Guitar Solo 2

San Francisco Bay Blues

Words and Music by Jesse Fuller

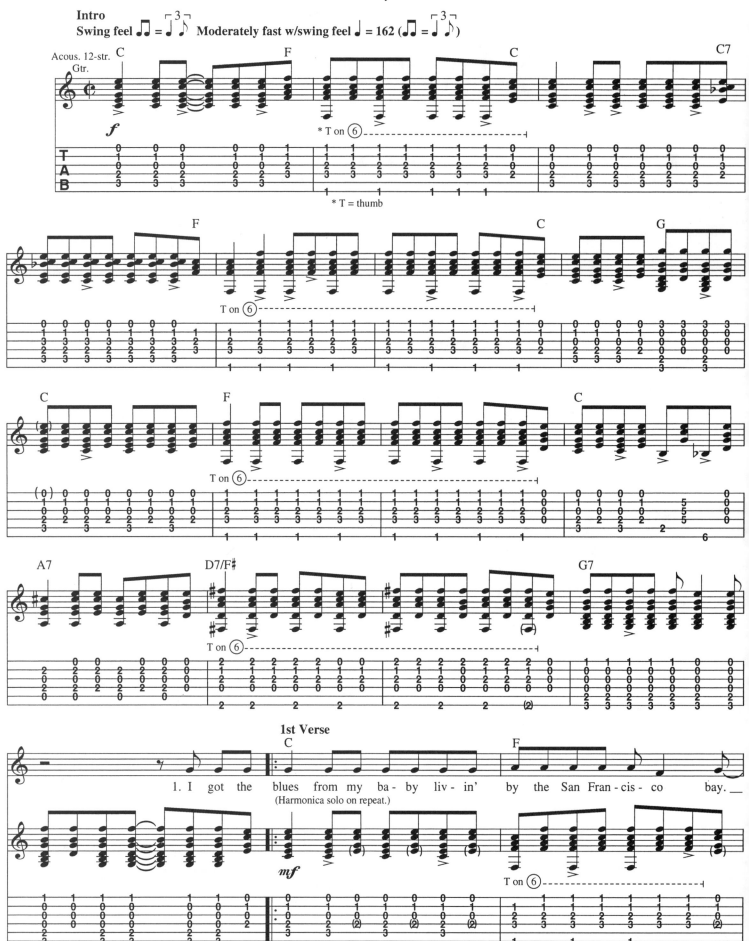

1. I got the blues from my ba-by liv-in' by the San Fran-cis-co bay.

(Harmonica solo on repeat.)

be an-oth-er brand new day, ____ walk-in' with (my) ba-by down ____

by the San Fran-cis-co bay. ____

3rd Verse

(Sit-tin') down, look-in' from a back door,

won-d'rin' which way to go. ____ (The) wom-an, I'm so

107

NOTATION LEGEND